# LIVERMUSH COOKBOOK

**WNC DELICACY**

Recipes by Darrell Rice
Photography by Morgan Rice

Livermush Cookbook
by Darrell Rice and Morgan Rice

www.livermushcookbook.com

©2018 Darrell Rice and Morgan Rice

All rights reserved. No portion of this book may be reproduced in any form without permission from the publisher, except as permitted by U.S. copyright law.

Printed by IngramSpark

ISBN-13: 978-0-692-14328-5 (Paperback)

"Livermush is delicious."
    -a sensible person

# Contents

## BREAKFAST 9
## SIDES & SNACKS 25
## LUNCH 45
## DINNER 65

# BASICS

# Livermush Spread

16 oz livermush, cut into a very small dice
6 tbsp mayonnaise
2 tbsp apple cider vinegar
½ tsp prepared horseradish (optional)
½ tsp worcestershire sauce

¼ tsp garlic powder
¼ tsp paprika
¼ tsp sugar

In a bowl, add all the ingredients and mix until you have a slight paste consistency. You can use a wooden spoon but you may find it a little easier using your hands.

**BASICS**

# Livermush Crumbles

1. Cut a 16oz block of livermush into small cubes
2. Place a tbsp of oil into frying pan and bring to medium heat
3. Stirring occasionally, cook livermush until pieces are browned and slightly crispy, allowing some pieces to break up

# Breakfast

# BREAKFAST

**BREAKFAST WHEEL** 11
**BREAKFAST PASTRIES** 13
**DOUGHNUT SANDWICH** 15
**LIVERMUSH WAFFLES** 17
**HOMERUN BRUNCH** 19
**BREAKFAST CASSEROLE** 21
**BAKED EGG** 23

# BREAKFAST

# Breakfast Wheel

 8 Servings

1 8 oz can crescent rolls
3 oz livermush crumbles (see pg 7)
4 eggs
1 cup shredded cheddar
½ yellow onion, chopped
2 oz diced pimentos
ketchup
olive oil

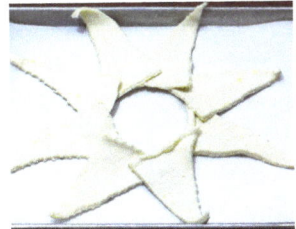

1. Preheat oven to 350°F and line a baking tray with parchment paper
2. Lay out the croissants as shown above with a small circle left in the middle
3. Grill onions with olive oil and mix with the livermush crumbles
4. Layer on the livermush mixture, top with half of the cheese, and a squeeze of ketchup
5. Use 3 eggs and cook to a scramble. Mix in the pimentos
6. Layer on top of the livermush mixture and top with the remaining cheese
7. Fold the ends of the croissants underneath
8. Beat the remaining egg and brush onto the top of the pastry
9. Bake for 15-20 minutes or until golden brown

# BREAKFAST

## Breakfast Pastries

---

● 4 Servings

---

8 slices livermush, fried
1 sheet frozen puff pastry
½ cup shredded colby jack cheese
8 thin slices roma tomato
8 oz thin sliced mushrooms

1 egg
olive oil
yellow mustard
salt

---

1. Preheat oven to 400°F
2. Pan fry mushrooms with a little olive oil and a pinch of salt, cooking until the liquid from the mushrooms has evaporated
3. Roll out puff pastry. Cut into 4 pieces, each should be 5" x 5"
4. As shown below, place 2 slices of livermush onto the pastry. Top with mustard, 2 slices of tomato, a quarter of the cooked mushrooms, and ⅛ cup shredded colby jack
5. Using a dab of water, pinch together the two side corners, as shown below
6. Place on a parchment lined baking tray
7. Whisk an egg and brush it onto the bare pastry
8. Bake for 20 minutes, or until golden brown

# BREAKFAST

# Doughnut Sandwich

 1 Serving

1 glazed doughnut
2 slices livermush
1 slice cheddar cheese
1 egg
1 tbsp maple syrup

1. Slice the doughnut in half creating a bun
2. Fry both slices of livermush in a pan
3. Once the livermush is cooked to your liking, melt a slice of cheese over the livermush
4. Place on the bottom side of the doughnut bun
5. Cook an egg to your liking
6. Place egg on top of livermush and cheese
7. Drizzle the maple syrup over the top

**BREAKFAST**

# Livermush Waffles

 8 Servings

2 cups flour
6 oz livermush crumbles (see pg 7)
2 cups milk
⅓ cup granulated sugar
2 eggs
½ cup vegetable oil
1 tsp vanilla extract
4 tsp baking powder

For sauce:
4 tbsp unsalted butter
2 tbsp grape jelly
1 tsp water

1. Mix the flour, sugar, and baking powder together
2. Combine the eggs, milk, oil, and vanilla in separate bowl
3. Gently combine the wet ingredients into the dry ingredients
4. Fold in the livermush crumbles
5. Make your waffles according to the instructions that accompany your waffle maker, making sure each waffle has a good portion of crumbles
6. To create sauce: over a gentle heat, combine the jelly, butter, and water until they melt and blend together.  The longer the the sauce stays on the heat, the more water you will need to add to keep its consistency

**BREAKFAST**

# Homerun Brunch

● 1 Serving

| | |
|---|---|
| 2 slices livermush | 1 egg |
| 2 slices bacon | 1 slice white bread |
| 1 sausage | 1 roma tomato |
| 5-6 mushrooms | 4 oz vegetarian baked beans |
| 1 hashbrown patty | salt and pepper |

The trickiest part of this brunch is ensuring that all the components are cooked together. Except for the toast and beans, this dish could be cooked in one frying pan. However, it becomes a lot more challenging when cooking more than one portion. A way to overcome this would be to bake some items and fry the others. Example:

1. Preheat oven to 400°F
2. Fry sausages in oil for a couple of minutes to get some color. Transfer to a parchment lined large baking tray and place in the middle of the preheated oven
3. Slice roma tomato in half and rub a little oil on each side and season with salt and pepper. Place on a small parchment lined baking tray. Place in oven below the sausages
4. Five Minutes after sausages have been cooking, add bacon to the tray and return to oven
5. Heat 1 tsp oil to a medium high heat in a non-stick frying pan and add mushrooms and a little salt. Cook until all the liquid released from the mushrooms has disappeared. Remove mushrooms from pan and add to the small baking tray and return to oven
6. Cook hashbrown according to package instructions
7. Remove the large baking tray from oven and flip the bacon and sausages over. Return to oven
8. If needed, add a little more oil to the frying pan and cook the livermush slices for approximately 4-5 minutes, flipping halfway through. Drain livermush on paper towel and add to small tray in the oven
9. Heat beans in a saucepan
10. Add a little more oil to the saucepan and cook the egg to your liking. Season with salt and pepper
11. Check the bacon after 20 minutes of going into the oven to make sure it is cooked, also check the sausages (internal temp of 160°F). Once cooked, remove all ingredients from the oven
12. Toast or broil bread to your liking
13. Place all ingredients onto a plate

**BREAKFAST**

# Breakfast Casserole

 8 Servings

16 oz livermush cubes or crumbles (see pg 7)
8 oz shredded cheddar
6 slices white bread
2 cups whole milk
8 eggs
2 tbsp yellow mustard
½ tsp salt
½ tsp pepper

1. Preheat oven to 350°F
2. Coat a 9" x 13" pan with cooking spray
3. Tear up the bread and put on bottom of the pan
4. Place the livermush and cheese on top of the bread pieces
5. In a bowl, beat the eggs with the mustard, salt, and pepper
6. Pour the egg mixture over the livermush, cheese, and bread
7. Bake for 40 minutes, until egg is set and cheese is golden on the edges

**BREAKFAST**

# Baked Egg

 1 Serving

½ oz livermush crumbles (see pg 7)
1 egg
3 cherry tomatoes, halved and lightly cooked
1 green onion, sliced at a bias
1 oz shredded cheddar
1 tbsp heavy cream
salt and pepper

1. Preheat oven to 350°F
2. Brush the inside of the ramekin with softened butter. Season with salt and pepper
3. Place 4 tomato halves, livermush crumbles, and onions into the bottom of the ramekin
4. Carefully break an egg into the ramekin and drizzle the heavy cream onto the egg, making sure to avoid the yolk. Sprinkle the cheese on top
5. Place the ramekin in a shallow roasting pan. Gently pour boiling water around the ramekin, coming up approximately 1 inch
6. Place in the oven and bake for 10 minutes, until the egg white is set with the yolk still runny. Bake for an extra 3 minutes for a more cooked egg
7. Garnish with remaining tomato halves and green onions

# Sides & Snacks

## SIDES & SNACKS

**LIVERMUSH, LEEK, AND CHEESE SAUSAGES** 27
**LIVERMUSH & BROCCOLI CASSEROLE** 29
**LIVERMUSH ROLLS** 31
**LIVERMUSH BRUSSEL SPROUTS** 33
**CREAM CHEESE & LIVERMUSH WONTONS** 35
**MUSHED POTATOES** 37
**MUSH MAC AND CHEESE** 39
**MUSHY EGGS** 41
**SCALLOPED POTATOES** 43

## SIDES & SNACKS

# Livermush, Leek, & Cheese Sausages

● 13 Servings

1½ cups shredded pepperjack cheese
3 oz livermush crumbles (see pg 7)
3 tbsp milk
1½ cups breadcrumbs
1 leek

2 eggs
¼ cup flour
1 tsp yellow mustard
vegetable oil

1. Slice and rinse the leek. Heat oil in a pan and cook leeks until they are tender. Allow to cool
2. In a bowl, mix together cheese, livermush crumbles, 1 cup breadcrumbs, sliced leek, 1 egg, and mustard. Slowly add milk until the consistency allows you to shape the sausages into 2 inch long shapes that hold together
3. Pour oil into the bottom of a pan and heat to medium high
4. Fill 3 separate bowls with flour, 1 egg, and ½ cup breadcrumbs
5. Take the sausages and first coat in flour, then coat in egg, and then coat in breadcrumbs
6. Once all of the sausages are coated, place them into frying pan
7. Cook each side for 2 minutes until they become golden brown. Rotate 3 times so that all sides get cooked. Total cook time should be between 8 and 10 minutes
8. Remove from pan and allow the excess oil to drip onto a plate covered with paper towels

**SIDES & SNACKS**

# Livermush & Broccoli Casserole

● 8-10 Servings

16 oz livermush crumbles (see pg 7)
1½ cups uncooked minute rice
1 large head of broccoli, roughly chopped
1½ cups shredded cheddar
1½ cups whole milk
1 cup celery, small diced
½ cup fresh parsley, finely chopped
1 medium onion, small diced
1 10.5 oz can cream of chicken soup
¼ tsp of pepper

1. Preheat oven to 350°F
2. In a large bowl, mix all ingredients well and transfer to a 9"x13" dish
3. Place in oven and bake for 30 minutes
4. Remove from oven

**SIDES & SNACKS**

# Livermush Rolls

● 24 rolls

12 oz livermush
12 oz ground pork sausage
1 egg, beaten
3 sheets puff pastry, approx. 6" x 10"

1. Preheat oven to 350°F
2. In a bowl, combine livermush and sausage and mix thoroughly
3. Divide into 3 even amounts
4. Roll each portion into a long sausage shape, approx 8 inches long
5. Place each sausage shape mixture onto each sheet of puff pastry
6. Carefully roll a sheet of puff pastry around each sausage shape, stopping 1 inch from the end of the sheet. Brush egg wash onto remaining inch of pastry and continue to roll. The egg wash will help seal the puff pastry
7. Tuck in the sides of the puff pastry and pinch all edges of the pastry together
8. Using a sharp knife, cut into 1 inch sections. Wipe the knife clean between cuts
9. Lightly score each piece and transfer to parchment lined baking tray
10. Lightly egg wash each piece
11. Bake approx 25 minutes or until pastry is golden brown
12. Can be served hot or cold

**SIDES & SNACKS**

# Livermush Brussel Sprouts

 4-6 Servings

16 oz brussel sprouts
3 oz livermush crumbles (see pg 7)
1 small red onion, sliced
2 tsp red wine vinegar
salt and pepper

1. Trim the ends of the sprouts and remove any loose leaves
2. Add a little oil to a frying pan and cook the red onion until soft. Add the red wine vinegar and livermush crumbles and cook until warmed through
3. Cook the sprouts in a large pan of salted boiling water for 5 minutes
4. Drain and mix into the livermush and onion mixure
5. Season with salt and pepper to taste

**SIDES & SNACKS**

# Cream Cheese & Livermush Wontons

● makes 35 wontons

35 wonton wrappers
½ cup finely chopped green onion
8 oz livermush crumbles (see pg 7)
½ cup cream cheese (at room temp)
canola oil

1. In a bowl, mix together the green onion, livermush, and cream cheese until it becomes a rough paste consistency
2. Place 1 tsp of mixture in the center of each wonton wrapper
3. Using your finger, rub some water on all four edges of the wonton
4. Fold the wonton in half, making sure to push the edges together firmly, creating a nice triangle pocket
5. Fill a pan with approx 1 inch oil and turn up to medium heat. All stovetops vary on temperature, so you may need to adjust accordingly. To test if the oil is ready, drop a piece of spare wonton wrapper in and see if it starts to fry
6. Using tongs, carefully place the wontons into the oil, making sure not to over load the pan. Fry to a golden brown, remove, and place on a paper towel covered plate to allow the oil to drain off
7. Serve with sweet chili sauce or other desired dipping sauce

**SIDES & SNACKS**

# Mushed Potatoes

 4 Servings

2 large potatoes, peeled and chopped
8 oz livermush crumbles (see pg 7)
200 ml half and half (gently heated)
2 tbsp unsalted butter, diced
salt and pepper

1. Place chopped potatoes into large pan of cold salted water and bring to a boil
2. Cook for 10 minutes or until tender
3. Drain the potatoes and put back into the pan. Place back onto hot stove for about one minute. This will remove the excess moisture from the potatoes
4. Add butter and gently mash gradually adding warm half and half
5. Try not to overwork the potatoes and only mash until all lumps are removed. Stir in any remaining half and half
6. Mix in the livermush and season with salt and pepper to taste

**SIDES & SNACKS**

# Mush Mac and Cheese

 6-8 Servings

8 oz livermush crumbles (see pg 7)
8 oz macaroni, cooked
10 oz shredded cheddar
2 cups half and half
½ cup breadcrumbs
3 garlic cloves, crushed
4 tbsp unsalted butter
2 tbsp flour
2 tsp worcestershire sauce
salt and pepper

1. Preheat oven to 350°F
2. Melt 2 tbsp butter in frying pan and add crushed garlic. Cook for 3 minutes, making sure the garlic does not burn
3. Add breadcrumbs and mix thoroughly. Set aside
4. Gently melt 2 tbsp butter in a saucepan. Once melted, gradually add 2 tbsp flour, whisking continuously, and cook for 1 minute
5. Slowly add 2 cups of half and half, whisking continuously. Cook until thickened
6. Stir in 10 oz shredded cheese until cheese has melted
7. Add the salt, pepper, and worcestershire sauce to the cheese mixture
8. Stir in macaroni and livermush
9. Transfer the macaroni, livermush, and cheese mixture to a 9" x 13" glass baking tray
10. Sprinkle the garlic and breadcrumb mixture over the top
11. Bake for 15-20 minutes

**SIDES & SNACKS**

# Mushy Eggs

 12 Servings

6 eggs, boiled and peeled
¼ cup mayonnaise
1½ oz livermush crumbles, cooked (see pg 7)
1 tsp apple cider vinegar
1 tsp yellow mustard
1 shallot, finely diced
½ jalapeno, seeded and finely diced
1 pinch of salt and pepper
paprika

1. In a bowl, crumble the livermush a little finer using your fingers
2. Add mayonnaise, vinegar, mustard, jalapeno, shallots, salt and pepper, and mix well
3. Slice the 6 eggs in half longways and remove the yolks. Add the yolks to the livermush mixture
4. Mix thoroughly
5. Using a piping bag, pipe the livermush mixture back into the eggs
6. Finish with a sprinkling of paprika

**SIDES & SNACKS**

# Scalloped Potatoes

● 3-4 Servings

2 large potatoes, peeled
4 oz livermush crumbles (see pg 7)
¾ cups cream
3 garlic cloves, unpeeled
1 tsp dried thyme
1 tsp salt
1 tsp pepper

1. Preheat oven to 325°F
2. Using a mandolin, thinly slice the potatoes and place in a bowl of water to stop discoloration
3. Using the flat side of a large knife, push down on each clove of garlic until it is slightly smashed
4. Add the garlic (including skins) to the cream and gently heat for 5 minutes. Remove garlic from cream. Discard garlic and add the salt and pepper. Set cream aside
5. Place a layer of the potatoes, slightly overlapping, into the bottom of a small casserole dish
6. Pour a layer of cream over the potatoes. Sprinkle a little of the livermush and thyme over the cream
7. Repeat until the potatoes are used up, approximately 2 more layers
8. Make sure the top layer isn't covered with any cream
9. Bake in oven for 1 hour

# Lunch

# LUNCH

**LIVERMUSH & ASPARAGUS QUICHE** 47
**SWEET POTATO MASH** 49
**CLUB SANDWICH** 51
**FLATBREAD** 53
**RICE STUFFED TOMATOES** 55
**LIVERMUSH "SCOTCH" EGG** 57
**CREAM OF LIVERMUSH SOUP** 59
**INDIAN SPICED STUFFED MUSHROOMS** 61
**B.L.L.T.** 62
**BROILED MUSH & CHEESE SANDWICH** 63

**LUNCH**

# Livermush & Asparagus Quiche

● 8 Servings

1 frozen deep dish pie crust
½ yellow onion chopped
1 cup chopped asparagus
6 oz livermush crumbles (see pg 7)
1 cup half and half
1 cup shredded swiss cheese

4 eggs
1 tbsp olive oil
½ tsp salt
½ tsp pepper
8 asparagus tips (optional)

1. Preheat oven to 375°F
2. Pan fry the onion and asparagus with the olive oil
3. Mix together the onion, asparagus, livermush crumbles, and swiss cheese
4. Place the mixture into pie crust
5. Beat together eggs, half and half, salt, and pepper
6. Pour egg mixture over ingredients in pie crust
7. Lightly pan fry 8 asparagus tips and place on top of quiche
8. Bake for 40-45 minutes until egg is set

# Sweet Potato Mash

 4 Servings

2 sweet potatoes, washed and scrubbed
6 oz livermush crumbles (see pg 7)
1 oz walnut pieces
2 tsp cinnamon
2 green onions, chopped

1. Preheat oven to 425°F
2. Prick sweet potatoes with a fork and place on a parchment lined baking tray. Place in oven and bake for 45-50 minutes, until tender
3. Remove from oven and cut in half longways. Carefully scoop out the flesh, making sure to not break the skins
4. Place the flesh into a mixing bowl
5. Heat the livermush crumbles and add to the mixing bowl, along with the walnut pieces and cinnamon
6. Mix well and then scoop the mixture back into the skins
7. Top with chopped green onions and serve

# LUNCH

# Club Sandwich

● 1 Serving

4 slices livermush, pan fried until crispy
4 slices bacon, cooked
3 slices bread, toasted
2 slices smoked turkey
8 slices roma tomato
2 leaves romaine lettuce, washed
1 egg, over easy
mayonnaise
8 toothpicks

1. Take the first slice of toast, spread with mayonnaise and layer with lettuce, 4 slices tomato, 2 slices bacon, 2 slices livermush, and 1 slice turkey
2. Place another slice of toast on top and slightly push down
3. Repeat layers, this time topping with the egg
4. Push down a little with the last piece of toast and hold together with 4 toothpicks.  Slice diagonally into 4 pieces
5. Carefully remove each slice and place another toothpick through the bottom to secure all layers

# LUNCH

# Flatbread

 4 Servings

4 flatbreads or naan breads
livermush spread (see pg 6)
1 cup shredded cheddar cheese
20 cherry tomatoes, halved
12 slices fresh buffalo mozzarella
fresh baby arugula
extra virgin olive oil
pepper

1. Preheat oven to 350°F
2. Cover the bread with a layer of livermush spread
3. Sprinkle ¼ cup shredded cheddar over each flatbread
4. Distribute 10 tomato halves and 3 mozzarella slices for each flatbread
5. Sprinkle with pepper
6. Bake for approximately 8-10 minutes
7. Finish with fresh baby arugula and a drizzle of extra virgin olive oil

**LUNCH**

# Rice Stuffed Tomatoes

 2 Servings

2 large tomatoes
¼ cup basmati rice
½ cup water
½ cup green onion
½ cup livermush crumbles (see pg 7)
¾ cup shredded cheddar
salt and pepper
olive oil

1. Preheat oven to 350°F
2. Place ¼ cup rice in saucepan. Pour small drop of oil in rice and mix around until all rice is lightly coated in oil. Pour ½ cup water into saucepan, put lid on, and turn on high heat. Once the water starts to boil, drop down to low temp and let cook for 15 minutes
3. Slice tops off of tomatoes and discard. Scoop out insides and place in food processor. Blitz well. Reserve ¼ cup of the blended tomato and discard the remainder
4. Dice green onion until you have approximately ½ cup total
5. In a bowl, mix together cooked rice, green onion, livermush crumbles, ½ cup shredded cheddar, ¼ cup blended tomato, and salt and pepper to taste
6. Place the hollowed out tomatoes onto parchment lined baking tray
7. Stuff the tomatoes with the rice mixture until they are fully stuffed
8. Top each one with ⅛ cup shredded cheddar
9. Bake for 15 minutes

# LUNCH

# Livermush "Scotch" Egg

 4 Servings

4 eggs, boiled and peeled
8 oz livermush, diced very small
4 good quality bratwurst, approximately 8 oz
1 beaten egg
4 tbsp flour
1 oz plain breadcrumbs
1 oz finely crushed salt and vinegar chips
pepper

1. Fill a fryer with oil and preheat to 300°F
2. Remove the skins from the bratwurst and mix the meat with the livermush
3. Divide into 4 equal portions
4. Using your hands, make a patty large enough to encase the egg
5. Take each boiled egg and wrap it in the meat patty, making sure it encases the egg entirely
6. Take 3 bowls and in the first bowl, add the flour along with a pinch of pepper. In the second bowl, add the beaten egg. In the third bowl, combine the breadcrumbs and crushed chips
7. With each meat wrapped egg, coat in the flour, next in the egg, and finally in the breadcrumb mixture, ensuring an even coating. Repeat with the remaining eggs
8. Place the eggs carefully in the fryer and cook for 8-10 minutes, until golden brown and cooked through

**LUNCH**

# Cream of Livermush Soup

● 3-4 Servings

1 lb potatoes, peeled and diced into approximately ½ inch cubes
8 oz livermush crumbles, plus extra for garnish (see pg 7)
3 cups good quality chicken stock
½ cup heavy cream, plus extra for garnish
2 leeks, trimmed, cleaned, and thinly sliced (white and light green part only)
1 clove garlic, crushed
2 tbsp unsalted butter
1 tsp salt

1. In a large pot, soften the leeks and garlic in butter on a medium heat for 8-10 minutes, stirring occasionally
2. Add the stock and potatoes and bring to a boil
3. Turn down the heat to a simmer and cook for further 15 minutes, or until potatoes are cooked
4. Turn off heat and add livermush crumbles. Using a stick blender, pulse to a smooth texture. For an even smoother soup (pictured), push the soup through a fine sieve with a wooden spoon. Finish pushing the final coarser pieces through using a bowl scraper
5. Gently reheat the soup and stir in ½ cup cream
6. Transfer to bowls and finish with a swirl of cream and livermush crumbles

# LUNCH

# Indian Spiced Stuffed Mushrooms

● 4 Servings

8 oz livermush crumbles (see pg 7)
8 oz canned chopped tomatoes with green chilies
4 portobello mushrooms, whole
1 onion, finely sliced
1 cup ricotta cheese
6 cherry tomatoes, sliced in half
4 oz spinach
½ head of garlic, peeled and roughly chopped
1½ oz ginger root, skin scraped off and roughly chopped

3 tbsp heavy cream
2 tsp garam masala
1 tsp salt
½ tsp chili powder
2 tsp sunflower oil
2 tbsp water

1. Preheat oven to 350°F
2. Cook spinach in a large pan of salted boiling water for 2 minutes. Drain. Transfer to a food processor and blend to a paste. Set aside
3. Add garlic and ginger with 2 tbsp of water to a food processor. Blend to a paste.
4. Remove stalks from the mushrooms, and dice stalks very small
5. Heat the oil in a saucepan over medium heat and cook the stalks and onion for 10-12 minutes until brown, stirring occasionally
6. Remove the onion and mushroom mixture and drain on paper towels
7. Turn the heat to low then add the garlic and ginger paste and cook for 3 minutes, stirring often
8. Increase the heat to medium and add the tomatoes. Cook for 5 minutes
9. Add the livermush crumbles, spinach, onion and mushroom mixture, seasonings, and cook for 2 minutes
10. Stir in cream and cook for 1 minute. Remove from heat
11. Place the portobello mushrooms on parchment lined baking tray and bake for 10 minutes
12. Divide the mushroom stuffing into the 4 portobello mushrooms and top with ricotta cheese. Place tomato halves on top.
13. Return to the oven and cook for a further 10-15 minutes
14. Serve with basmati rice

# LUNCH

# B.L.L.T.

 1 Serving

2 slices white bread
3 slices livermush
3 slices bacon
3 slices tomato
lettuce
mayonnaise

1. Cook the livermush and bacon to your liking
2. Spread mayonnaise on each slice of bread
3. Build the sandwich with lettuce, tomato, bacon, and livermush

# LUNCH

## Broiled Mush & Cheese Sandwich

● 1 Serving

2 slices texas toast
1 slice tomato
2 oz livermush crumbles (see pg 7)
1 slice provolone
1 slice cheddar
worcestershire sauce

1. Toast each slice of bread on one side only
2. On one untoasted side of one piece of bread, place a slice of provolone and tomato
3. On the other untoasted side, add cheddar, a few dashes of worcestershire sauce, and livermush crumbles
4. Place each piece of bread under the broiler until the cheese is melted
5. Once cooked, remove from the heat and place the tomato and cheese toast on top of the livermush and cheese. Slice in half

# Dinner

# DINNER

**LIVERMUSH CARBONARA** 67
**LOBSTER SHELBY** 69
**ULTIMATE PORK CHOP SANDWICH** 71
**STUFFED CHICKEN** 73
**CELEBRATION MEATLOAF** 75
**SOUTHERN NACHOS** 77
**LIVERMUSH MANICOTTI** 79
**PESTO CALZONE** 81

**DINNER**

# Livermush Carbonara

● 4 Servings

12 oz linguini
16 oz livermush crumbles (see pg 7)
8 oz bacon, chopped
1 onion, diced
3 eggs
5 oz parmesan, grated
6 tbsp heavy cream
2 tbsp unsalted butter
1 tbsp olive oil
salt and pepper

1. Bring a pot of salted water to a boil and add the linguini. Boil for 10-12 minutes or until tender
2. Over a medium heat, melt the butter together with the olive oil. Add the onion and cook until softened
3. Add the bacon and stir frequently until cooked. Add the livermush crumbles and cook for 1 minute
4. In a separate bowl, mix the cheese, cream, eggs, salt, and pepper
5. Drain the linguini and return to pot
6. Add the cream mixture to the hot pasta and stir. The heat from the pasta will cook the mixture
7. Mix the livermush, bacon, and onions into the pasta

# Lobster Shelby

 2 Servings

2 lobster tails, 4-6 oz each, cooked
2 oz livermush crumbles (see pg 7)
1½ cups heavy cream
¼ tsp worcestershire sauce
1 egg yolk, lightly beaten
pinch of salt
parsley
lemon

1. Add the cream and worcestershire sauce to a saucepan and bring to a gentle boil, stirring constantly
2. Remove from the heat and add a small amout of the heated cream to the beaten egg yolk
3. Then combine the egg and cream mixture back into the rest of the cream
4. Bring to a gentle boil, stirring constantly, for 6 minutes or until thickened
5. Stir in livermush crumbles and a pinch of salt. Cook for a further 2 minutes
6. Remove from heat
7. Slice the 2 cooked lobster tails in half and remove the meat. Chop into pieces. Gently fold into the cream and livermush mixture
8. Put the mixture back into the tails and squeeze a little lemon juice over the top
9. Finish with finely chopped parsley

# DINNER

# Ultimate Pork Chop Sandwich

● 4 Servings

4 boneless pork chops
1-2 oz livermush spread (see pg 6)
8 oz plain breadcrumbs
½ cup coleslaw
4 sesame seed buns
4 slices beefsteak tomato

4 slices white cheddar cheese
4 romaine lettuce leaves
2 tbsp yellow mustard
4 tsp apple cider vinegar
ketchup
1 tbsp oil

1. Preheat oven to 350°F
2. Cut a deep pocket into each pork chop and stuff with the livermush spread
3. In a bowl, mix together the mustard and vinegar
4. Place the breadcrumbs in a separate bowl
5. Take a pork chop and coat with the mustard mixture. Then coat with the breadcrumbs. Repeat with the remaining pork chops
6. In a non stick frying pan, heat the oil to a medium heat and pan fry the pork chop 1 minute each side. Remove from pan onto parchment lined baking tray
7. Bake for 35 minutes or until pork temperature reads 150°F
8. Cut the buns in half and spread both sides with ketchup
9. Assemble the sandwiches by layering lettuce, tomato, pork chop, cheese, and coleslaw

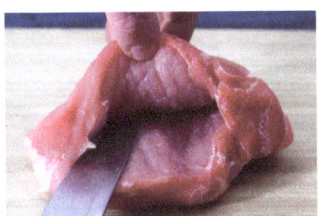

# DINNER

# Stuffed Chicken

● 4 Servings

4 chicken thighs (skin on)
4 oz livermush spread (see pg 6)
salt and pepper

1. Preheat oven to 350°F
2. Loosen the skin of the chicken thigh and create a pocket.  Push the livermush spread to fill the pocket
3. Season the skin with salt and pepper
4. Place on a parchment lined baking tray
5. Bake for 45 minutes to an hour, until internal temperature reaches 165°F
6. Serve with seasoned vegetables and potatoes

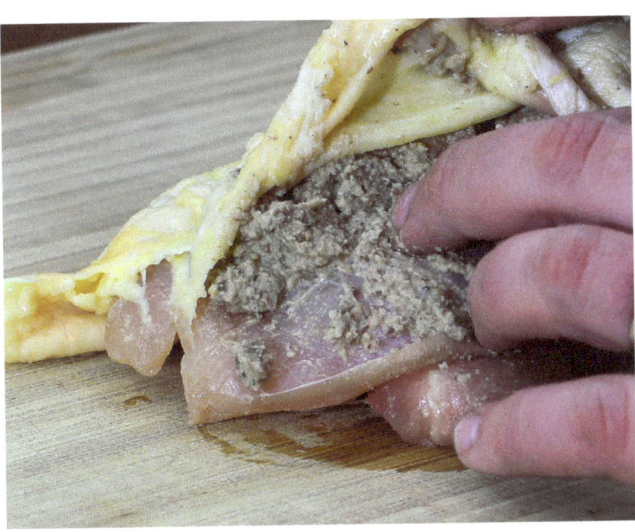

# DINNER

# Celebration Meatloaf

● 6 Servings

1 lb livermush, small dice
1 lb 85% lean ground beef
1 lb ground pork
8 oz plain breadcrumbs
2 granny smith apples, peeled, cored, grated
1 small onion, grated
1 cup grated parmesan
¼ cup sour cream
3 garlic cloves, crushed
2 eggs, beaten
6 tbsp carolina gold bbq sauce
1 tsp salt
½ tsp pepper

1. Preheat oven to 350°F
2. Take the grated onion and using your hands, squeeze out excess liquid
3. Except for the bbq sauce, put all ingredients into a large mixing bowl
4. Using your hands, mix thoroughly, ensuring that all the ingredients are evenly distributed
5. Line a 9.25" x 5.25" x 2.75" loaf pan with plastic wrap and fill the pan with the mixture. Be sure to press the mixture very firmly into the pan to ensure a less crumbly texture when cooked
6. On a parchment lined baking tray, turn out the meatloaf and remove the plastic wrap
7. Tightly cover the top and sides of the meatloaf with aluminum foil
8. Bake for 1 hour and 45 minutes
9. Remove the foil from the meatloaf and brush with 4 tbsp of bbq sauce
10. Cook for a further 15 minutes, or until internal temperature reaches 160°F
11. Remove from the oven and let the meatloaf stand for 15 minutes
12. Brush the meatloaf with the remaining bbq sauce before slicing and serving

**DINNER**

# Southern Nachos

● 4 Servings

1 bag tortilla chips
2 cups shredded cheddar
1 can corn
1 can blackeye peas
½ red onion diced
9 oz livermush crumbles (see pg 7)
guacamole

1 cup sour cream
2 tbsp barbecue sauce
2 oz diced pimentos
2 roma tomatoes diced
chopped parsley
chopped green onion
pinch of salt

1. Preheat oven to 350°F
2. Lay chips onto parchment paper lined baking tray
3. Layer on 1½ cups cheese, livermush, corn, peas, and pimentos. Finish with ½ cup cheese
4. Bake for 10 minutes
5. Mix together bbq sauce and sour cream with a pinch of salt
6. Remove from oven and place in serving tray. Top with tomatoes, onion, and bbq sour cream
7. Garnish with parsley and green onion
8. Serve with guacamole

# DINNER

# Livermush Manicotti

 4 Servings

8 cooked manicotti shells
16 oz livermush spread (see pg 6)
15 oz jar alfredo sauce
1 cup shredded mozzarella
7 oz jar sundried tomatoes in olive oil

1. Preheat oven to 400°F
2. Mix ½ cup shredded mozzarella with the livermush spread
3. Using your fingers, stuff the livermush mix into the cooked manicotti shells until they are fully stuffed
4. Pour half the jar of alfredo onto the bottom of a 9" x 13" baking pan
5. Lay the stuffed shells on top of the sauce
6. Sprinkle ¼ cup cheese on top of the shells
7. Pour the remaining alfredo on top
8. Lay the sundried tomatoes on top and sprinkle with remaining cheese
9. Cover the pan with aluminum foil and bake for 30 minutes

# DINNER

# Pesto Calzone

 2 Servings

2 12" fresh pizza crusts (unbaked)
8 oz livermush crumbles (see pg 7)
8 oz fresh mozzarella ball
5 oz shredded parmesan
2 oz walnut pieces
6 oz grape tomatoes (approximately 15)
3½ oz pesto
1 egg

1. Preheat oven to 425°F
2. Roll out pizza doughs on parchment papers
3. Slice tomatoes in half
4. In a bowl, mix cold livermush crumbles, pesto, walnuts, tomato halves, and parmesan cheese
5. Pour half of the mixture on one half of each crust, making sure to keep a 1 inch distance from the edges
6. Slice the mozzarella and place 3 slices on top of each mixture
7. Fold the crust over to make the calzone and pinch the crust together on the edges using your fingers
8. Brush with egg wash and put 2 slits along the top
9. Bake for 20 minutes until golden brown

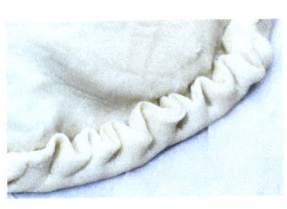 

| | |
|---|---|
| BREAKFAST WHEEL | 11 |
| BREAKFAST PASTRIES | 13 |
| DOUGHNUT SANDWICH | 15 |
| LIVERMUSH WAFFLES | 17 |
| HOMERUN BRUNCH | 19 |
| BREAKFAST CASSEROLE | 21 |
| BAKED EGG | 23 |
| LIVERMUSH, LEEK, AND CHEESE SAUSAGES | 27 |
| LIVERMUSH & BROCCOLI CASSEROLE | 29 |
| LIVERMUSH ROLLS | 31 |
| LIVERMUSH BRUSSEL SPROUTS | 33 |
| CREAM CHEESE & LIVERMUSH WONTONS | 35 |
| MUSHED POTATOES | 37 |
| MUSH MAC AND CHEESE | 39 |
| MUSHY EGGS | 41 |
| SCALLOPED POTATOES | 43 |
| LIVERMUSH & ASPARAGUS QUICHE | 47 |
| SWEET POTATO MASH | 49 |
| CLUB SANDWICH | 51 |
| FLATBREAD | 53 |
| RICE STUFFED TOMATOES | 55 |
| LIVERMUSH "SCOTCH" EGG | 57 |
| CREAM OF LIVERMUSH SOUP | 59 |
| INDIAN SPICED STUFFED MUSHROOMS | 61 |
| B.L.L.T. | 62 |
| BROILED MUSH & CHEESE SANDWICH | 63 |
| LIVERMUSH CARBONARA | 67 |
| LOBSTER SHELBY | 69 |
| ULTIMATE PORK CHOP SANDWICH | 71 |
| STUFFED CHICKEN | 73 |
| CELEBRATION MEATLOAF | 75 |
| SOUTHERN NACHOS | 77 |
| LIVERMUSH MANICOTTI | 79 |
| PESTO CALZONE | 81 |

www.ingramcontent.com/pod-product-compliance
Lightning Source LLC
Chambersburg PA
CBHW042051290426
44110CB00001B/26